A Tree in the Garden

A new vision...

by

Miriam Oren and Peninnah Schram
Illustrated by Alice Whyte

To Rose,
For a better tomorrow!
Miriam Oren

Nora House

Cover and book design by Miriam Oren

Art by Alice White

Published by Nora House
9122 White Eagle Court
Raleigh, NC   127617
oren2a@yahoo.com

If you are unable to order this book from your local bookseller, you may order directly from the publisher.

Library of Congress Control Number: 2004092345
Printed in Korea

ISBN 0-9752958-0-2

Dedicated to my grandchildren,
Alex and Danielle

It is written that God created the
world and saw that it was good.

Since I create my world, I too,
choose to see it as good.

Miriam Oren

Dedicated to my grandchildren,
Dorielle, Aaron, and Ilan

....Therefore I choose life...
Deuteronomy 30:19

Peninnah Schram

Dedicated to openness and
understanding, and the harmony that
proceeds from them.

Alice Whyte

Foreword

This book, inspired by the biblical story in the book of Genesis 1-3, celebrates the first woman's great contribution to humanity. Unlike the traditional interpretation which portrayed God's displeasure with humans and led to their expulsion from the Garden, this new vision portrays a loving relationship and deep bond between the first humans, Isha and Ish,* and God.

Miriam and Peninnah

See explanation of the names in the Notes section on page 50.

A Tree in the Garden

*A new vision...acknowledging the wisdom,
courage, and foresight of the first woman.*

Eager to reach the great gathering of God's creatures, Shayna glided gallantly, forging a narrow path in the dense forest undergrowth.

Gracefully, she wove her way under fallen trees and over gnarled roots. Her shiny skin flickered, toying with the shimmering rays as they broke through the lush green treetops.

Her heart swelled when her eyes gazed on the multitude that had gathered to learn about her Great Grandfather, and the role he had played in shaping the destiny of humankind.

At this time, when humans look at snakes as villains, Shayna felt compelled to retell the deeds of her ancestor.

After all, it was her Great Grandfather who had revealed the path of knowledge to the first humans, and unraveled the mystery of God's warning regarding the Tree of Knowledge.

Upon spotting Shayna, the assembly swiftly cleared a path to welcome her in. Even the old sycamore tree above the clearing beckoned her to nestle among its stretched-out limbs.

Effortlessly, Shayna moved up the tree and coiled her long body around a thick, white branch, whisper-hissing, "Thisss isss good!"

"It is wonderful to see so many of you here. I know you have traveled from far and near to hear Great Grandfather's story. Though there are many versions of what happened in the Garden of Eden, it is from my tongue that you will hear the story of creation as it truly happened."

A hush came over the assembly, as Shayna began to tell her story.

Out of chaos, God created the heavens and the earth. The sun did not yet shine in the heavens and the stars did not yet twinkle, so God said, "Let there be light." And God saw that it was good. And there was evening and there was morning, a first day.

On the second day, God separated the waters above from the waters on earth, and gathered the waters and formed the oceans and the rivers and the dry land. And the rain came down from heaven, awakening what was within the earth.

On the third day, God commanded the earth to spring forth with every kind of grass, herb, and fruit tree. And God saw that it was good.

On the fourth day, God created the sun to rule the day and the moon and the stars to rule the night.

On the fifth day, God created fish of all kinds to fill the waters and fowl of all kinds to fly in the sky.

On the sixth day, God created the beasts of the earth, the cattle, and all other creatures. And God saw that it was good.

But God's best creation was yet to come. And God said, "Let Us form humans in Our image," to entrust them with the world, to explore, and share in the joy of the newly created world.

And in the image of God, Ish and Isha, the first man and woman, were created. God commanded them to have children so that humans would forever inhabit the earth. Satisfied that it was very good, God blessed the world and all living things, and there was evening and there was morning, a sixth day.

Having completed the work of creation, God admired how beautiful and perfect everything was.

Pleased, God rested on the seventh day.

Among God's creation was the lush, green Garden of Eden, which God designated as home to Isha and Ish. They lived there harmoniously with the other inhabitants of the Garden. Not a worry crossed their minds, since all their needs were provided for them, except for one.

On a day like many other days, Ish was playfully chasing a butterfly. While the butterfly rested on a fragrant white blossom of a citrus tree, Ish carefully approached the butterfly with his hands cupped. The butterfly was almost within Ish's reach, when it spread its wings and flew to a nearby rosebud.

The butterfly stopped for a moment, admired its beauty, and off it flew toward the blazing purple iris. Flitting from flower to flower, with Ish in pursuit.

Suddenly, the butterfly soared toward the heavens, fluttered its wings and reverently bowed to a princely tree. For all the Garden inhabitants knew the secret this tree held, only Isha and Ish were not yet told. In a gentle glide, the butterfly flew away, out of Ish's sight.

Searching for the butterfly, Ish realized that he had wandered off to an unfamiliar area of the Garden.

Exploring his new surroundings, Ish noticed the majestic tree, radiant with a quiet beauty, as it stood alone in the clearing.

Tired and hungry from chasing the butterfly, the fruit hanging from one of the branches of the tree looked appetizing. Stretching from his toes to his fingertips, Ish reached for the sun-sweetened fruit, when suddenly he heard God call his name. "Ish! You are free to eat of every tree in the Garden except from this one, the Tree of Knowledge of Good and Bad. Beware, for once you eat from the fruit of this tree, your life in the Garden will end."

Forgetting all about his hunger, Ish ran to tell Isha about God's warning.

Months went by, and Isha and Ish continued their carefree life in the Garden. Each morning after a long night, Isha and Ish got up; they ate, played, ate, and again went to sleep.

One afternoon while picking fruit near the Tree of Knowledge, Isha came upon Great Grandfather basking on a rock, soaking up the warmth of the sun. Lazily, Great Grandfather glanced up and saw Isha picking fruit from surrounding trees, except from the Tree of Knowledge.

Leisurely, Great Grandfather crawled up a tree trunk not far from where Isha was picking mulberries.

14

His plump body was not as agile as it used to be – he was old even then – but his seasoned eyes had a kind and warm gaze. Softly, not to startle Isha, he hissed, "Tell me, why did you pick the fruit from all of the other trees but not from this one?"

Wide-eyed, she exclaimed, "God told Ish that if we ate from or touched that tree, our life in the Garden would end."

Great Grandfather gently assured Isha, "What God told Ish is true, that if you ate from this tree, your life in the Garden will end. However, that does not mean that your life will end.

On the contrary, if you choose to taste of this fruit, a whole new life will be waiting for you. Your eyes, your mind, and your heart will be opened making it possible for you to see, think, and feel wondrous things."

Perplexed, Isha asked, "If that is so, then why did God forbid us to eat from this tree?"

"But, God did not forbid you to eat the fruit of this tree. What God did is warn you of what would happen if you did."

"I do not understand."

"What God meant is that once you eat from the fruit of the Tree of Knowledge of Good and Bad, you will receive a remarkable gift, the freedom to choose the kind of life you want to live."

"I still do not understand," she said.

"Don't you see, my child, that there is something special about this tree?"

"No," replied Isha.

"Tell me, Isha, why do you pick the fruits from all the other trees?"

"That is a silly question! To eat when I am hungry or thirsty."

"So," said Great Grandfather, "God planted all the fruit trees, the herbs, and the grasses to feed you and the other creatures in this Garden."

"Yes," said Isha. "Hmm, I am really confused. If that is so, then why did God warn us not to eat from the Tree of Knowledge of Good and Bad."

"Because the fruit from this tree is not food for the body."

"Then, what is it for?"

"God created the fruit of this tree specially for you to feed your mind and soul," whispered Great Grandfather wistfully.

"Mind and soul? What are those?"

"That is what you might discover," answered Great Grandfather. "Even though God provided the tree for you and Ish, the choice to have the power to shape your own destiny is up to you."

Confused, Isha sat on the grass amidst the lush verdant growth of the Garden to ponder on what she had just been told. She was startled when Great Grandfather asked, "Tell me Isha, what do you do all day here in the Garden?"

"Lots of things. From the time the sun wakes and until it goes to sleep, Ish and I never stop. We play hide-and-seek with the animals, roll down the hill, throw stones in the river, and splash in the water. When we get hungry, we pick raspberries, my favorite, and other fruits — except from this one tree, of course."

"So you do whatever you please."

"I guess I do," replied Isha.

"Do you ever wonder what else there might be to do in this world, outside the Garden?" asked Great Grandfather.

Puzzled, Isha asked, "Is there something else to do? And what do you mean by 'in this world, outside the Garden?'"

Great Grandfather was pleased as he saw the seed of curiosity take hold and answered kindheartedly, "A whole new-world awaits you outside the Garden. A place to explore, to discover, and where new ideas are eager to be born. However, to be able to do all these things, you will need something only humans can possess."

"What is it?"

"It is knowledge."

"How is it that only humans can have knowledge?" asked Isha.

"Because only humans were created in God's image," replied Great Grandfather.

"What do you mean when you say 'created in God's image,' and what is knowledge?"

"After you taste the fruit of the Tree of Knowledge, you will soon begin to understand. However, only after you embark on your journey in search of knowledge, will you discover the answer to these questions."

24

Isha approached the tree, examined its fruit, and wondered if she would like its taste. She wanted to know how this fruit would change her.

Great Grandfather coiled himself between Isha and the tree and said, "I can tell from your eyes that you have become intrigued by the hidden secret of the fruit. But, before you decide to pick the fruit from this tree, I must warn you that knowledge is not easy to obtain. And once you have it, you have to know how to use it in good ways and not in bad ways."

Isha asked pensively, "How do I get this knowledge, and how will I learn to use it in good ways and not in bad ways?"

"That will be an important part of your journey."

Hesitantly, Isha asked. "But, but . . . what about God's warning?"

Weaving his way around the exposed, gnarled roots of the tree, Great Grandfather approached the trunk, nodded toward the shimmering sweet fruit and said, "Isha, God warned you about this tree for a reason. God did not want you to taste from the fruit of this tree without first thinking about what you were doing. God wanted you to choose carefully the kind of life you want to live. Because, once you eat from this fruit, your mind will be awakened and you will no longer look at the world with the innocence of a child and the Garden can no longer be home to you."

"How will I change and why will I have to go? And...and where will I go to?" asked Isha worriedly.

"With knowledge comes understanding, which will give you the ability to reflect and the freedom to choose. You will see things differently and discover hidden secrets that will make it seem as if you have entered a new world. The old Garden will seem as if you have left it a thousand paces behind.

With passage of time you will learn that the quest for knowledge is never-ending and forever you will be on a journey exploring God's wonderful creations."

Isha stood up stoically and decisively said, "I want to have this knowledge and learn all I can. I want to be able to make decisions that will make God proud."

Not convinced that Isha understood the consequences of her choice, Great Grandfather pleaded with her, "Think one hundred and one times whether or not you really want this knowledge, and whether you are ready to accept the consequences of your choice."

He warned Isha, over and over again. "To gain knowledge it takes a lot of hard work and, at times, it is difficult to choose between what is good and what is bad. However, in choosing knowledge, the rewards would be endless."

Looking up, Isha spotted an inviting branch. Climbing with ease, Isha sat down, leaned against the trunk, and shut her eyes. She needed to think about what Great Grandfather had told her. She heard Great Grandfather tell her that in choosing knowledge there would be, at times, pain and hard work, but in her heart she knew that the gift of choice and the joy of knowledge were worth it.

30

Although life in the garden was fun,
she was curious about what lay beyond.

Thankful for having been told the secret it held, Isha marveled at the Tree of Knowledge as never before. Isha knew that the future was in her hands, and was ready to accept the consequences of her choice. "I have made up my mind," whispered Isha.

Cautiously, Isha approached a branch, laden with the sweet, sun-bathed fruit, and plucked one. As she took a deep breath, her whole being filled with its sweet aroma. Hesitating for a moment, Isha slowly bit into it. With the sweet juice dripping down her chin, Isha murmured, "I did not know knowledge could be so delicious."

Meanwhile, on the far side of the Garden, after picking his favorite black grapes, Ish went looking for Isha. He spotted her in the clearing and discovered her eating from the fruit of the Tree of Knowledge.

Frantically, he yelled, "Isha! Isha! What are you doing?"

Isha explained, "Do not worry Ish, I now understand God's warning that if we eat from the Tree of Knowledge, our lives in the Garden would end. Since we did not know that there is a life outside the Garden, we misunderstood God's warning and thought that we would die."

Shocked, Ish asked, "What do you mean by life outside the Garden?"

Isha then gave a detailed account of her long conversation with Great Grandfather. Finishing her tale, Isha turned to Great Grandfather, "Did I leave anything out, my dear friend?"

Great Grandfather turned to face Ish and said, "Ish, what Isha told you is all true. Now you, too, have a choice to make. Do you want to share in the knowledge, and be able to choose good from bad? Do you wish to explore the world outside of the Garden?

Or do you want to remain in the comfort of what is familiar to you?"

Isha's eyes reflected what was in her heart, and Ish could not help but notice the sparkle and excitement in them. He stood quietly for a moment as a twinge of sadness overcame him at the thought of leaving behind all that had been his world. He looked around the Garden to take in its beauty, wanting to remember it forever. He looked into Isha's eyes again and he knew then what he had to do. Ish reached out to Isha's extended hand, took the fruit, and, with a little trepidation, tasted it.

The sweet juice awakened the thirst for knowledge that lay dormant within his soul, and his eyes and his mind opened wide to let in all that was new to him.

Suddenly the two began to tremble, realizing the enormity of their actions and the responsibility that comes with the knowledge of being divinely created.

Isha turned to Ish and said, "Now I begin to understand what it means to be created in God's image. What a grand legacy has been bestowed upon us."

"Indeed," replied Ish.

Gazing into Isha's eyes, Ish said tenderly, "You realize that in choosing to eat this fruit, we have chosen to leave the Garden and all its comfort?"

"Yes, I know. And although I feel a little frightened about going into the new world, I am also excited about the discoveries awaiting us."

As Isha and Ish gazed at the Garden for the last time, a tiny tear ran down Ish's cheek.

A sudden rush of wind startled them. Frightened, they ran and hid behind a tree.

"Where are you?" God called out.

"Here we are," answered Isha and Ish. "We did not realize it was You."

"Since you have eaten from the Tree of Knowledge of Good and Bad, you know you will have to leave the Garden of Eden. Life outside the Garden will not always be easy for you, and you may not always have the knowledge to choose wisely."

Following a moment of silence, God continued "But, remember that I will always be within you to guide you and guard you.

Isha and Ish, although you have chosen a difficult road, you have chosen well. How else would you ever begin to know Me or yourselves?

You will find that the search for knowledge is endless, but it is an exciting path to follow, full of wonder and discovery – and yes, some pain."

Tenderly, God continued, "When I created the world, I created this tree hoping that some day, when you were ready to explore the world outside this Garden, you would eat of its fruit. It is my special gift to you. It is the only possession you will need to guide you and your children through the challenges to come. Be good, kind, just, and

42

compassionate to each other, and most of all, remember that of all My creations, only you were created in My image."

Isha and Ish thanked God for their new life, for the gift of knowledge, and for not making them like the other creatures of the earth. Looking toward the heavens, they whispered, "Blessed be God day by day."

Breathlessly Isha turned to Ish and said, "All this time we have received blessings from God, and now, for the very first time, we have blessed God. We now have the power to bless each other, and everyone around us!"

And God saw that it was very good!

As Isha and Ish were leaving the Garden, Great Grandfather was waiting for them at the gate.

"I come to bid you farewell. When you think of me, think of me kindly. Do not regard me only as a crawling creature, but rather as one who has shown you how to emerge from darkness into light. With the gift of knowledge that you now possess, you can reach the top of any mountain. Using your imagination, you can fly anywhere. God created this wonderful world and gave it to you. Take good care of it. May a wonderful life be yours as you embark on your journey."

Gazing into Great Grandfather's kind eyes, Isha and Ish thanked him and blessed him for guiding them out of darkness into light.

As Great Grandfather bade them farewell, he let out a long, sad sigh, knowing that he could never join Isha and Ish on their journey.

He watched Isha and Ish walk out of the Garden, hand in hand, as they began their journey.

Finishing her story, Shayna looked down at the still, hushed gathering and she too sighed.

"That was the last time Great Grandfather saw Isha and Ish."

Gently, Shayna glided down from the comforting perch on the old tree and disappeared into the forest, forging a new path on her way to tell the story again.

Notes

Shayna means beautiful in Yiddish, the language spoken by Eastern European Jews and their descendants.

Isha (_   ) and Ish (_) mean woman and man in Hebrew, the ancient language of the Bible. These names were chosen because they contain within them the name of God, reinforcing the belief that we were created in God' image. When written in Hebrew, Isha and Ish differ by two letters (_), which spell out a form of God's name. (Pronunciation guide for Isha and Ish: In both names the capital I should be read as a long "e". In Ishá the accent is on the second syllable.)

There are passages in this story, which may raise questions for discussion:

– Who else is there when God says "Let Us form humans in Our image?"

– Why, when God told Ish that if he ate the fruit, his life in the Garden would end, did Isha say to the snake, "God told Ish that if we ate from it or touched that tree, our life in the Garden would end?"

Those passages, borrowed from the original story in the book of Genesis, have perplexed scholars through the ages. While nobody knows the answers for sure, they are open to varied interpretations.

About the Authors

Miriam Oren resides with her husband in North Carolina. She has always been a dreamer and acknowledges her husband to be her dream-maker. They are the proud parents of Phil and Ruth, and doting grandparents. Miriam considers herself a late bloomer, graduating from college at the age of fifty. Education has always been and still is a driving force within her. Her interests include travel, dance, and time spent reflecting. She attributes her inspiration and source of strength to her late mother, Nora.

Peninnah Schram is an internationally known storyteller, author of seven books of Jewish folktales, and a recording artist. She is an Associate Professor of Speech and Drama at Stern College of Yeshiva University. Peninnah is a recipient of numerous awards including the prestigious Covenant Award for Outstanding Jewish Educator and the National Storytelling Network's 2003 Lifetime Achievement Award.

Peninnah first heard stories from her parents. Her father, a cantor, told her biblical stories, while her mother shared the proverbs and folktales of the Jewish people. These stories filled her with the love of story and their wisdom. These lessons continue to resonate in her.

About the Artist

Alice Whyte learned her craft at her artist-mother's knee and studied interior design at UCLA. This is her second leap into creating art that interprets a story with a spiritual side.

She was thrilled to illustrate this beautiful non-traditional story of a "girl's" coming of age in an ancient garden. The experience of working with authors of different faith and traditions led her to discover that sisters are waiting to be found in every life experience.

Alice shows her artwork at various galleries in North Carolina.